MAZ
FOR KIDS

Dr Gareth Moore B.Sc (Hons) M.Phil Ph.D
is an Ace Puzzler, and author of lots of puzzle books.
He created an online brain-training site called BrainedUp.com,
and runs an online puzzle site called PuzzleMix.com. Gareth has
a PhD from the University of Cambridge, where he taught
machines to understand spoken English.

Buster Books

First published in Great Britain in 2021
by Buster Books, an imprint of Michael O'Mara Books Limited,
9 Lion Yard, Tremadoc Road, London SW4 7NQ

The material in this book was previously published in
The Kids' Book of Mazes and *The Kids' Book of Mazes 1*

 www.mombooks.com/buster Buster Books @BusterBooks @buster_books

Illustrations by John Bigwood and Sarah Horne

Puzzles designed and typeset by Dr Gareth Moore
www.drgarethmoore.com

Layout designed by Barbara Ward

A CIP catalogue record for this book is available from the British Library.

ISBN: 978-1-78055-836-3

1 3 5 7 9 10 8 6 4 2

Papers used by Buster Books are natural, recyclable products made of wood from
well-managed, FSC®-certified forests and other controlled sources. The manufacturing
processes conform to the environmental regulations of the country of origin.

Printed and bound in November 2021 by CPI Group (UK) Ltd,
108 Beddington Lane, Croydon, CR0 4YY, United Kingdom

MIX
Paper from
responsible sources
FSC® C020471

Contents

Amazing Mazes!

Amazing Mazes!

Mazes are puzzles that absolutely anyone can solve. They come in loads of different shapes and sizes, and all you need to complete them is a pen or pencil.

Find your way

A maze may look like a simple puzzle, but it can be very tough to solve. The mazes in this book are made up of branching passages through which the solver – that's you! – must find a route, from the 'In' to the 'Out'.

Whether the pathways in a maze are rectangular, triangular, hexagonal or circular, the walls are fixed, so you cannot jump over them. If you come to a dead end, you can only turn around or go back to the beginning and try again.

As some mazes may take you more than one try to solve, you might want to use a pencil so you can rub out your lines if you need to start again. But you can use a pen if you are feeling more confident.

Are you a beginner or the best?

The mazes in this book get tougher as the book progresses. There are four separate difficulty levels, which are shown at the top of each page. There's also a 'Time' line where you can fill in exactly how long it has taken you to solve each maze.

How to solve a bridge maze

A bridge maze is a type of maze that includes bridges. This allows the solution path to cross over and under itself. Have a look at this example, which shows how bridges work. They can make a maze a lot trickier to solve, and it's much easier to miss a potential route.

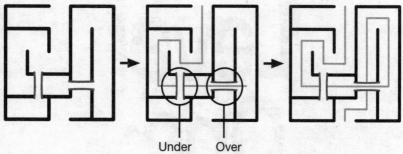

Under a bridge   Over a bridge

Introducing the Puzzle Master, Dr Gareth Moore

Dr Gareth Moore B.Sc (Hons) M.Phil Ph.D, who created the bridge and circular mazes in this book, is an Ace Puzzler, and author of lots of puzzle and brain-training books.

He created an online brain-training site called BrainedUp.com, and runs an online puzzle site called PuzzleMix.com. Gareth has a PhD from the University of Cambridge, where he taught machines to understand spoken English.

Level One:
Beginners

Maze 1

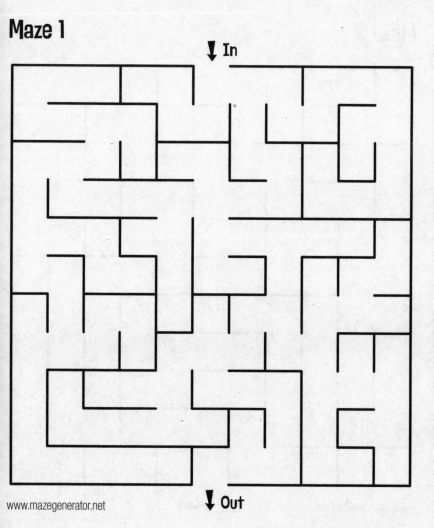

↓ In

↓ Out

www.mazegenerator.net

Time

 BEGINNERS

Maze 2

↓ In

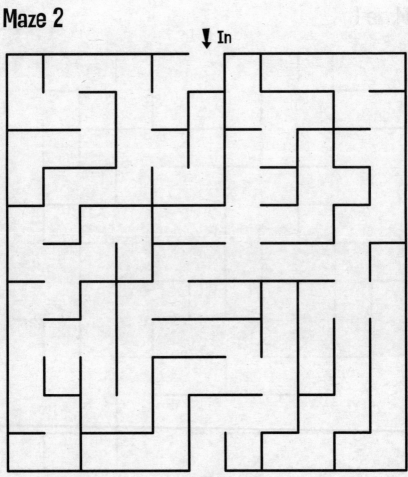

↓ Out

 Time ....

Maze 3

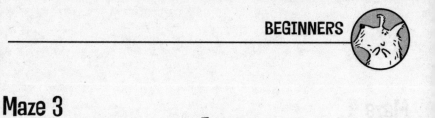

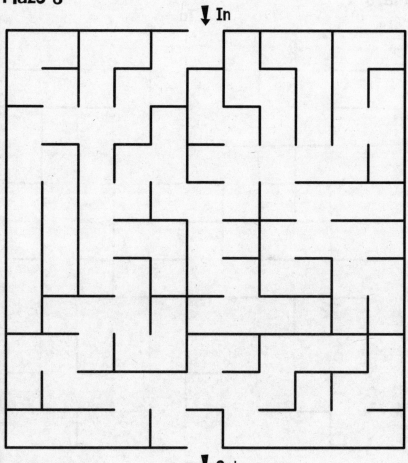

Time ....

Maze 4

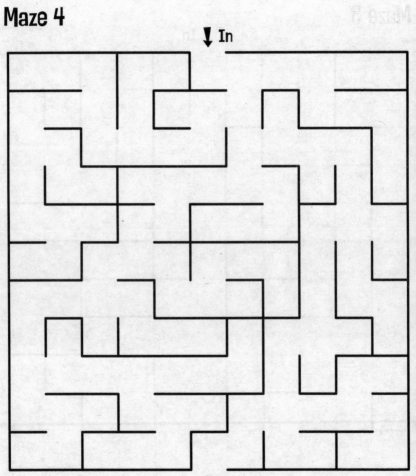

 Time ....

Maze 5

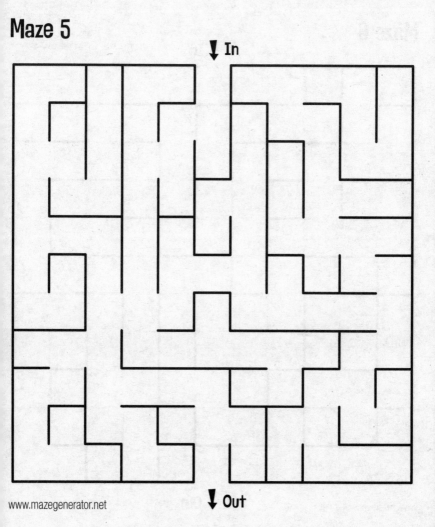

↓ In

↓ Out

Time ....

Maze 6

↓ In

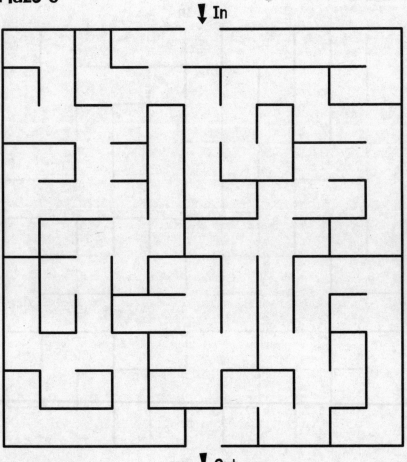

↓ Out

 Time ....

Maze 7

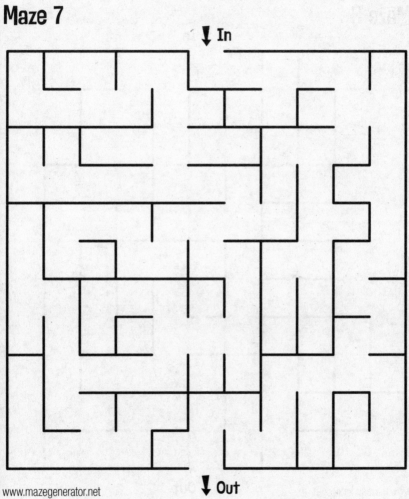

Time ....

Maze 8

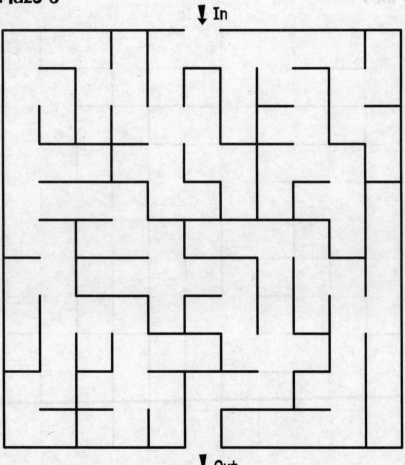

Maze 9

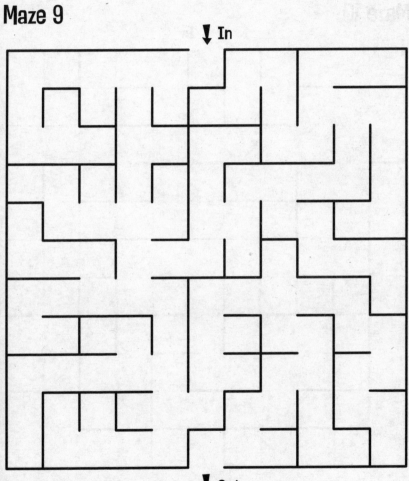

Time ....

Maze 10

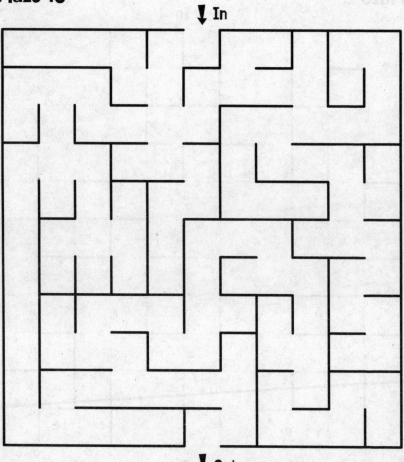

 Time ....

Maze 11

▼ In

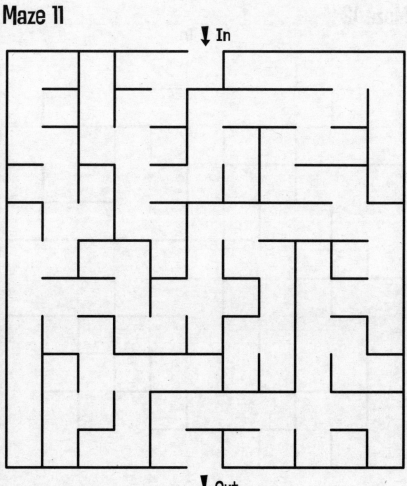

▼ Out

Time ....

Maze 12

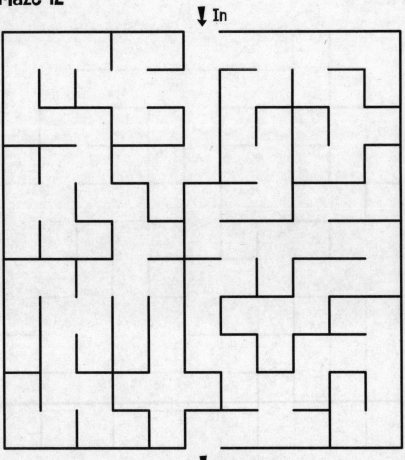

 Time ....

Maze 13

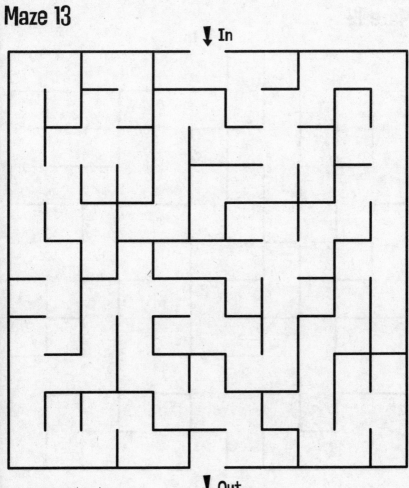

Time ....

Maze 14

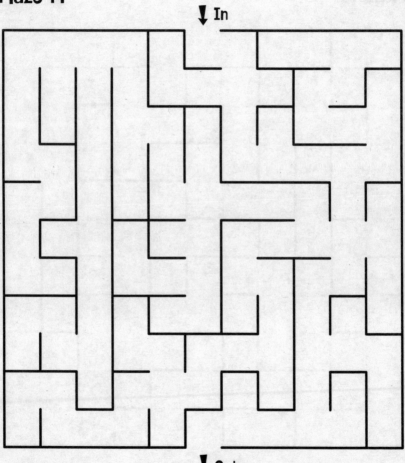

↓ In

↓ Out

⏱ **Time** ....

Maze 15

 In

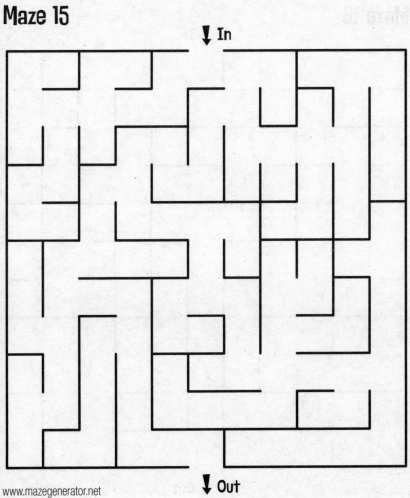

Out

Time ....

Maze 16

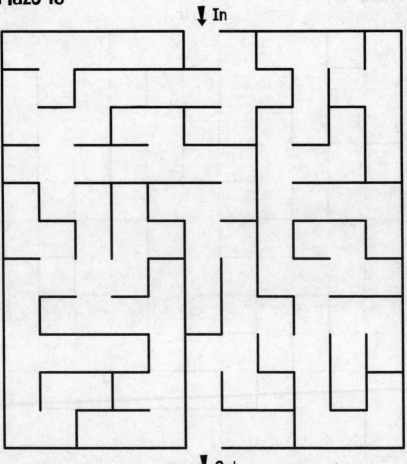

In

Out

 Time ....

Maze 17

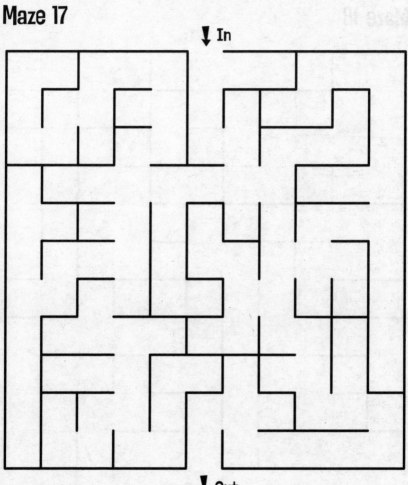

Out

Time ....

Maze 18

↓ In

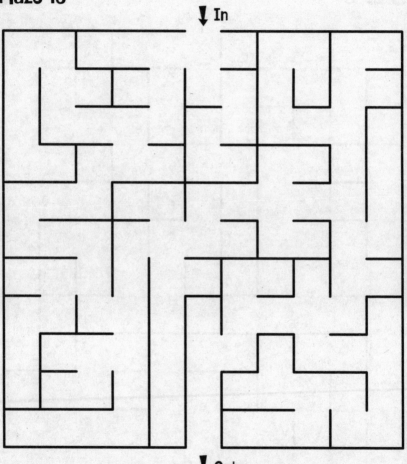

↓ Out

 Time ....

Maze 19

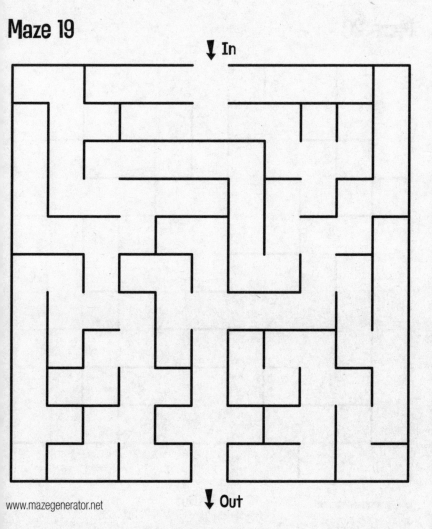

Time ....

Maze 20

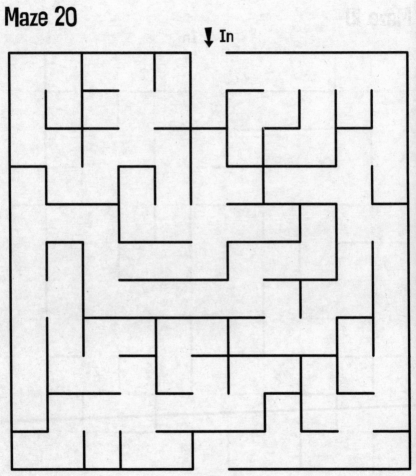

In

Out

 Time ....

Maze 21

In

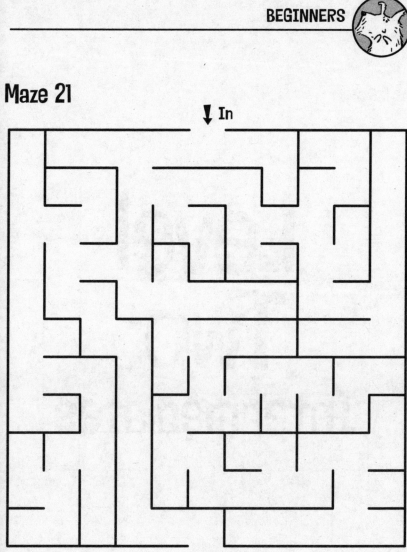

Out

Time ....

Level Two:
Intermediates

Maze 22

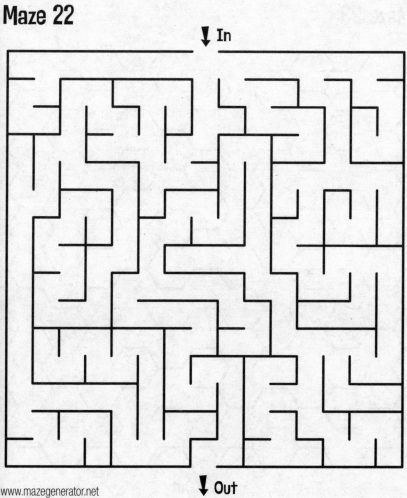

Time ....

Maze 23

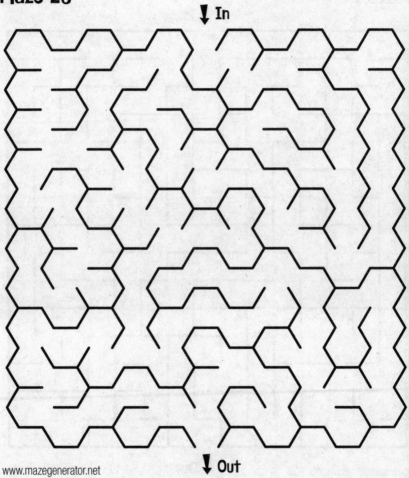

↓ In

↓ Out

🕐 **Time** ....

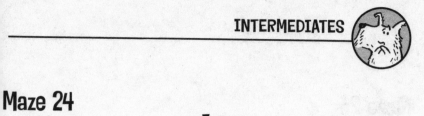

Maze 24

Time ....

INTERMEDIATES

Maze 25

↓ In

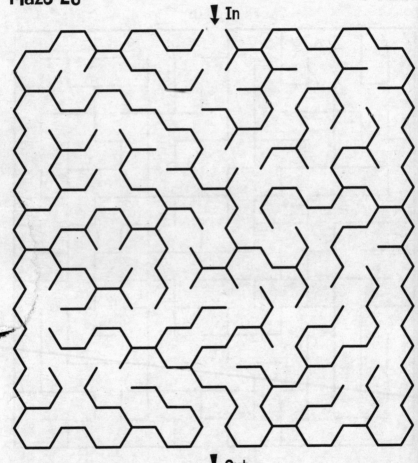

↓ Out

 Time ....

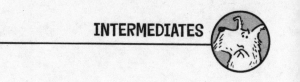

Maze 26

↓ In

↓ Out

Time

Maze 27

In

Out

Time

Maze 28

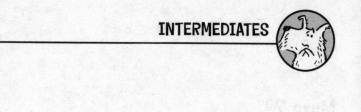

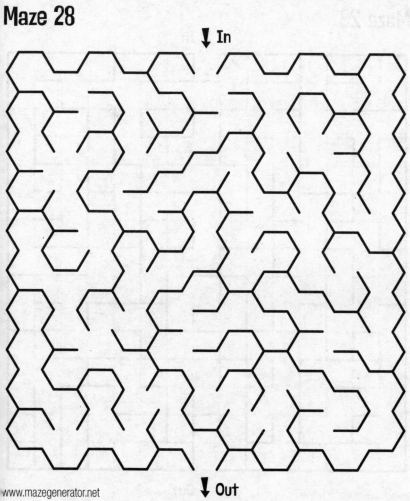

Time ....

INTERMEDIATES

Maze 29

www.mazegenerator.net

🕐 **Time** ....

Maze 30

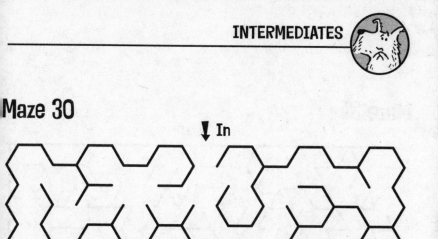

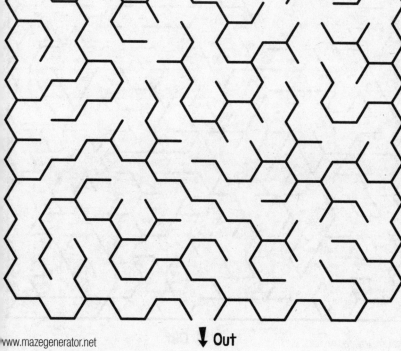

Time ....

Maze 31

▼ In

▼ Out

 Time ....

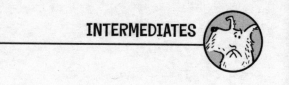

Maze 32

Time ....

Maze 33

 Time ....

Maze 34

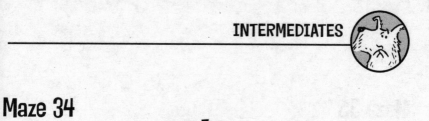

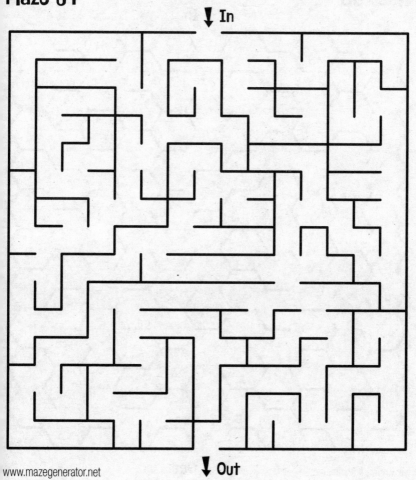

www.mazegenerator.net

Time _____

INTERMEDIATES

Maze 35

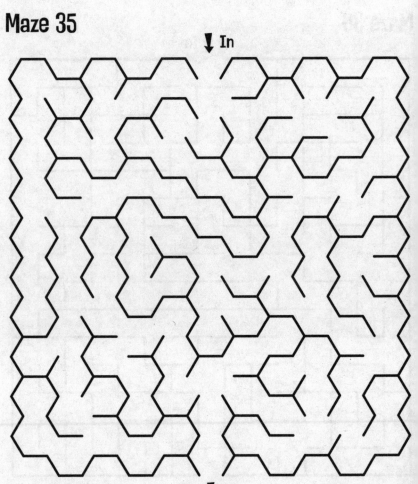

 Time ....

Maze 36

▼ In

▼ Out

Time ....

INTERMEDIATES

Maze 37

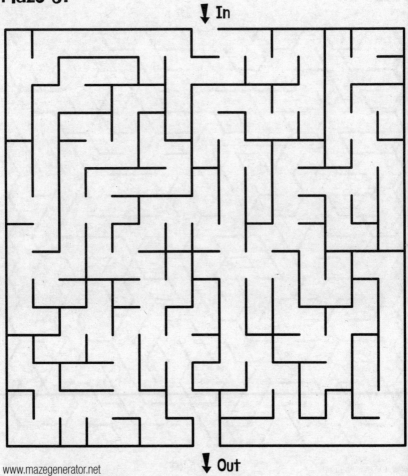

🕐 **Time**

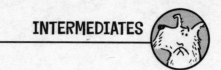

Maze 38

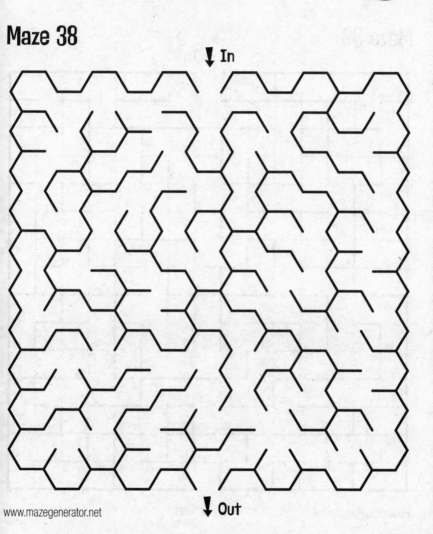

↓ In

↓ Out

Time ....

Maze 39

 Time ....

Maze 40

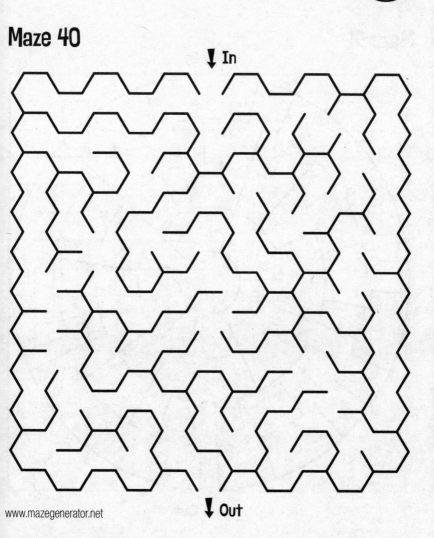

Time ....

Maze 41

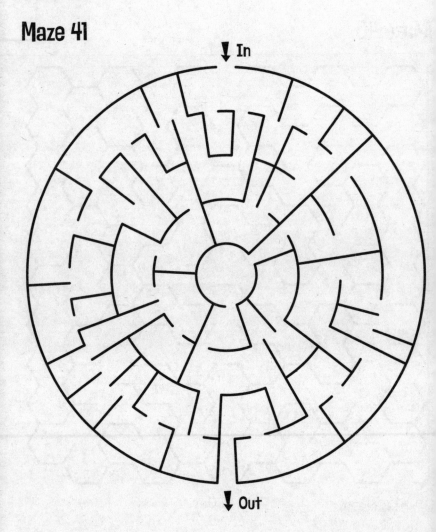

↓ In

↓ Out

 Time ....

Maze 42

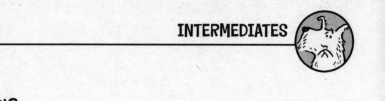

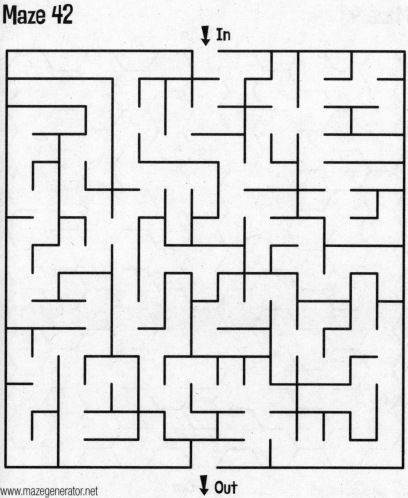

Time ....

INTERMEDIATES

Maze 43

↓ In

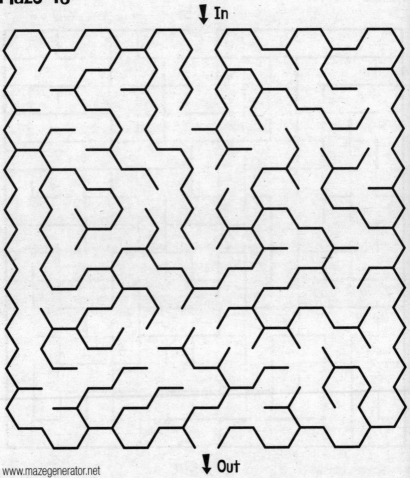

↓ Out

🕐 Time ....

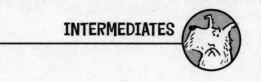

Maze 44

↓ In

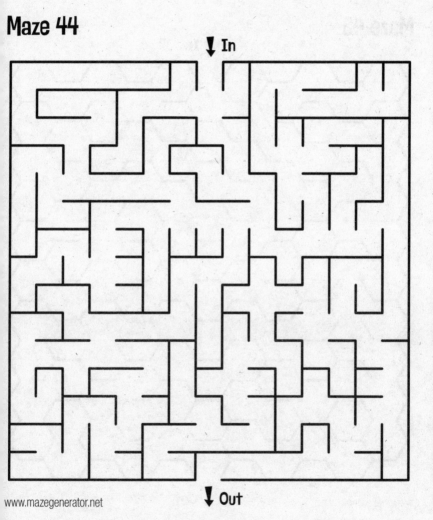

↓ Out

Time ....

Maze 45

↓ In

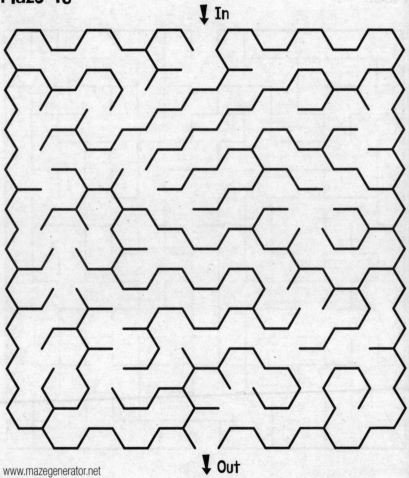

↓ Out

  Time ....

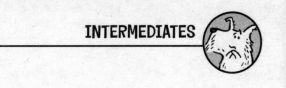

Maze 46

Time

 INTERMEDIATES

Maze 47

 Time..............................

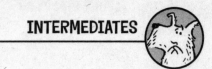

Maze 48

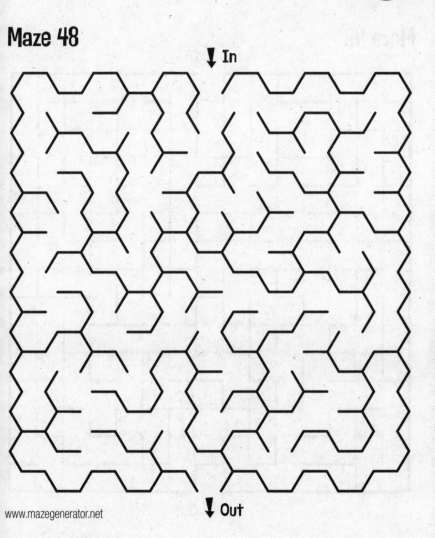

↓ In

↓ Out

Time ....

Maze 49

↓ In

↓ Out

 Time

Maze 50

↓ In

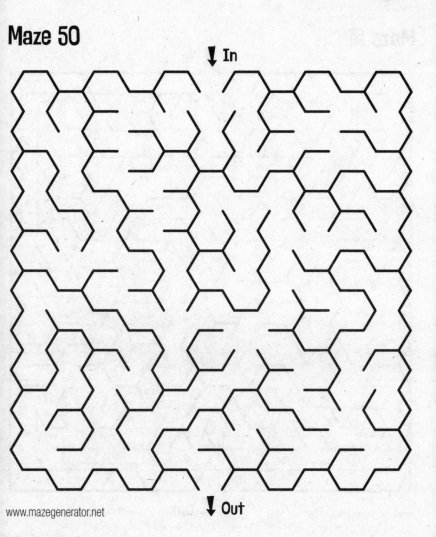

↓ Out

Time ....

Maze 51

In

Out

www.mazegenerator.net

Time ....

Maze 52

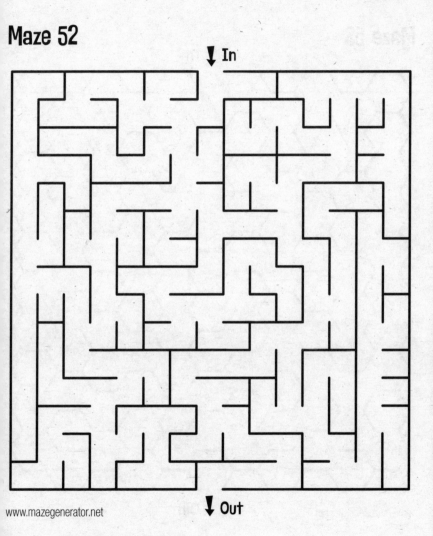

Time ....

 INTERMEDIATES

Maze 53

↓ In

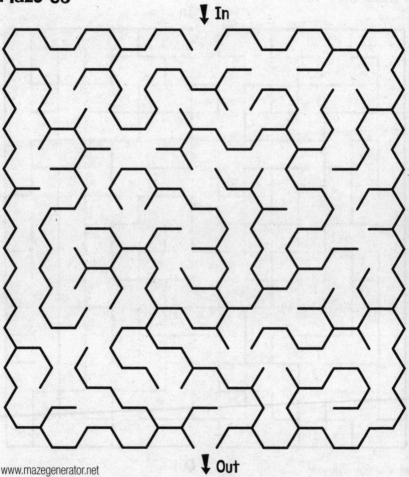

↓ Out

 www.mazegenerator.net

🕐 Time ....

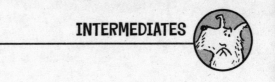

Maze 54

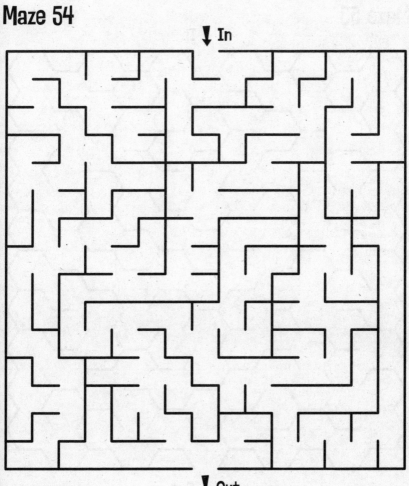

▼ In

▼ Out

Time ....

Maze 55

↓ In

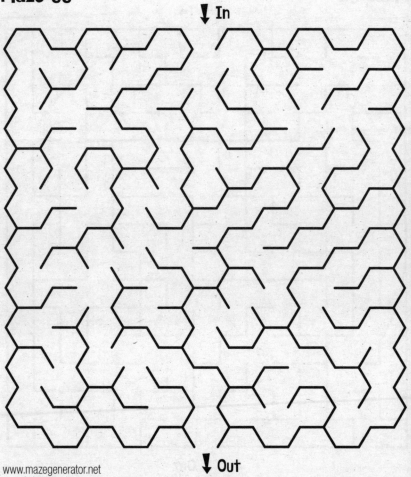

↓ Out

 Time ....

Maze 56

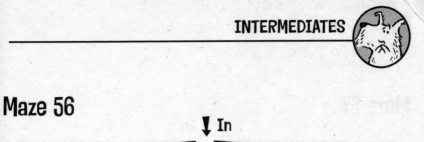

Time................................

Maze 57

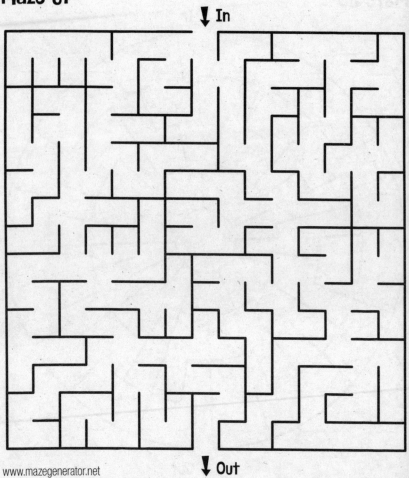

🕐 **Time**..

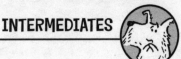

Maze 58

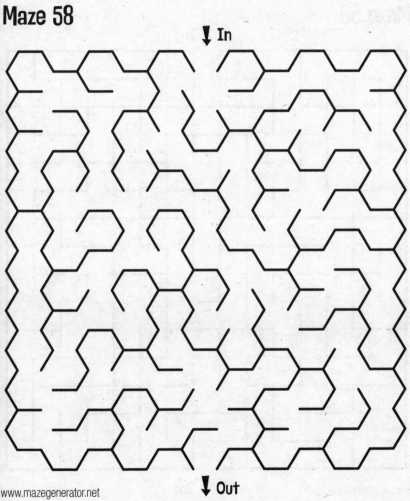

Time................................

Maze 59

↓ **In**

↓ **Out**

 Time ....

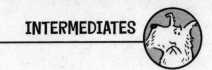

Maze 60

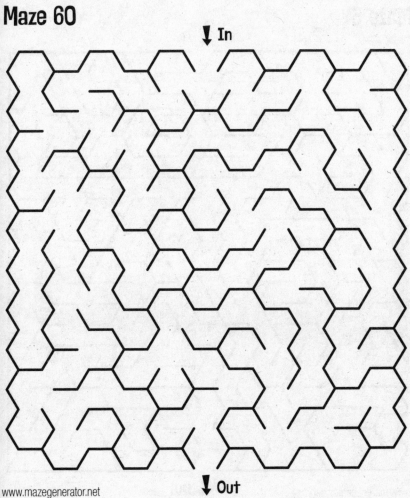

↓ In

↓ Out

Time

Maze 61

 Time ....

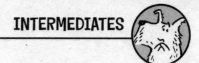

Maze 62

Time ....

Maze 63

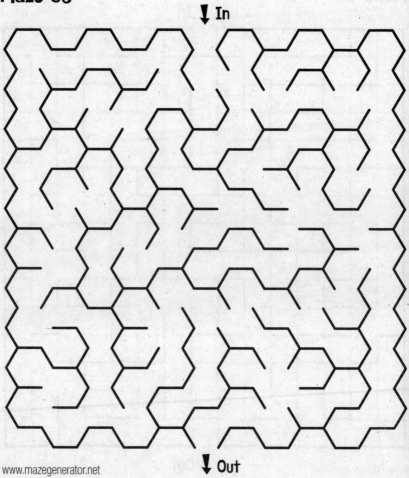

Time ....

Maze 64

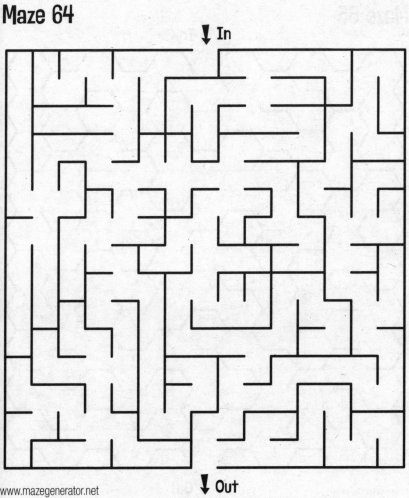

Time ....

Maze 65

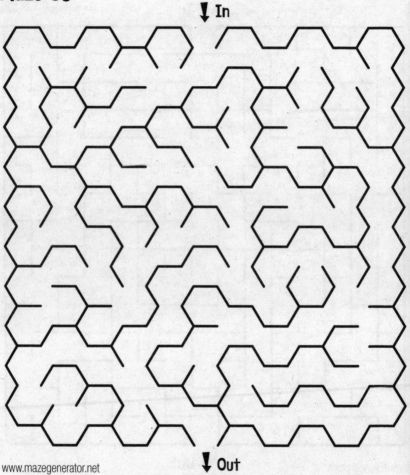

Time ....

Maze 66

↓ In

↓ Out

Time ....

INTERMEDIATES

Maze 67

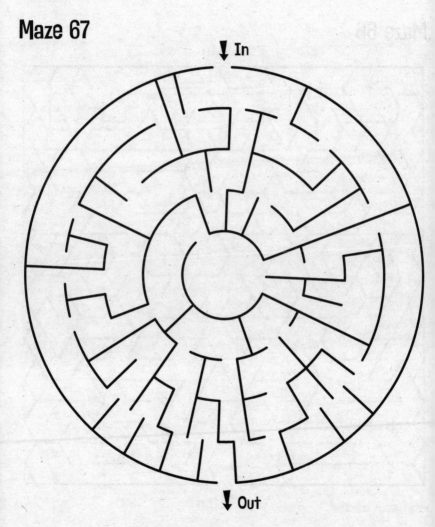

 Time ....

INTERMEDIATES

Maze 68

In

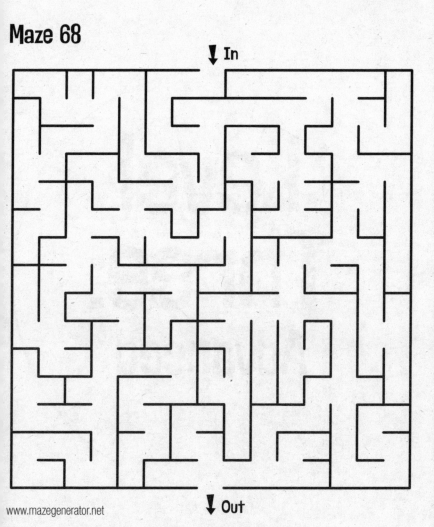

Out

Time

Level Three:
Advanced

Maze 69

Time ....

Maze 70

↓ In

↓ Out

Time ....

Maze 71

In

Out

Time

Maze 72

↓ In

↓ Out

 Time ....

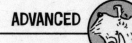

Maze 73

Time ....

Maze 74

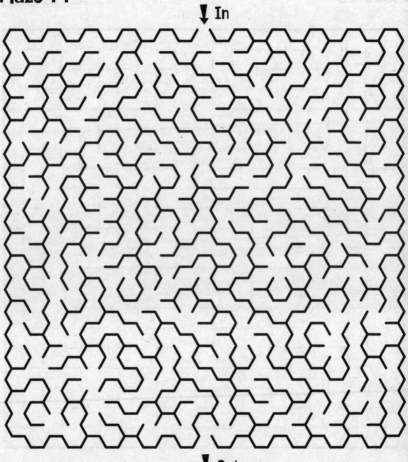

 Time ....

Maze 75

↓ In

↓ Out

Time

Maze 76

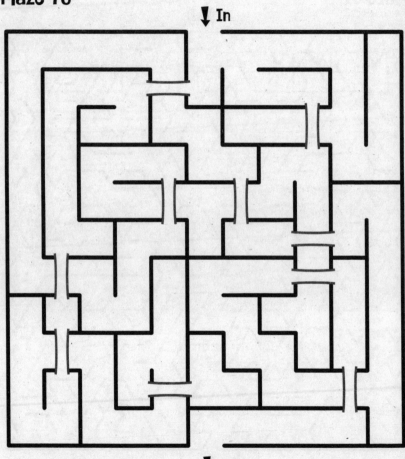

Maze 77

↓ **In**

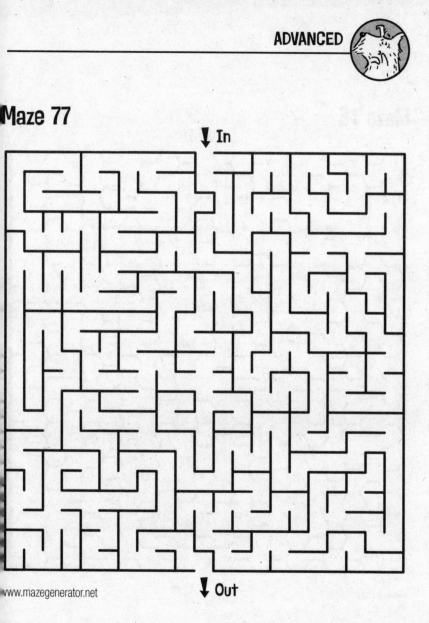

↓ **Out**

Time ....

Maze 78

In

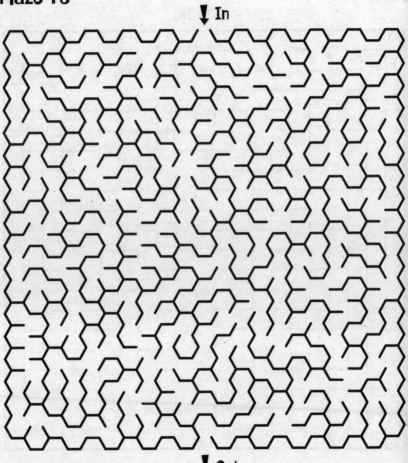

Out

 Time...

Maze 79

↓ **In**

↓ **Out**

Time ....

Maze 80

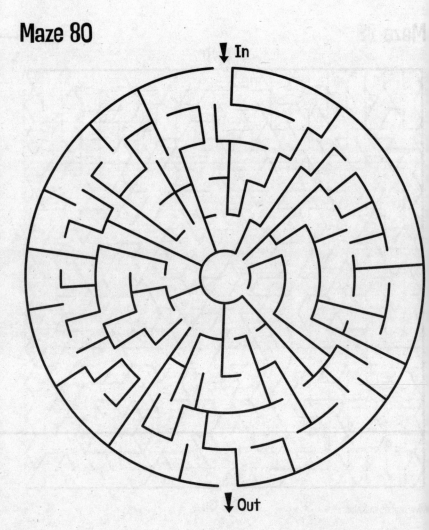

↓ In

↓ Out

 Time ....

Maze 81

In

Out

www.mazegenerator.net

Time ....

Maze 82

In

Out

Time ....

Maze 83

↓ In

↓ Out

Time ....

ADVANCED

Maze 84

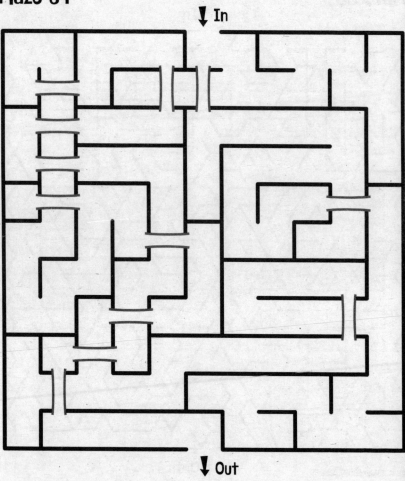

 Time ....

ADVANCED

Maze 85

In

Out

www.mazegenerator.net

Time ....

ADVANCED

Maze 86

In

Out

 Time

Maze 87

In

Out

Time ....

ADVANCED

Maze 88

 Time ....

Maze 89

↓ In

↓ Out

Time ....

Maze 90

In

Out

 Time ....

Maze 91

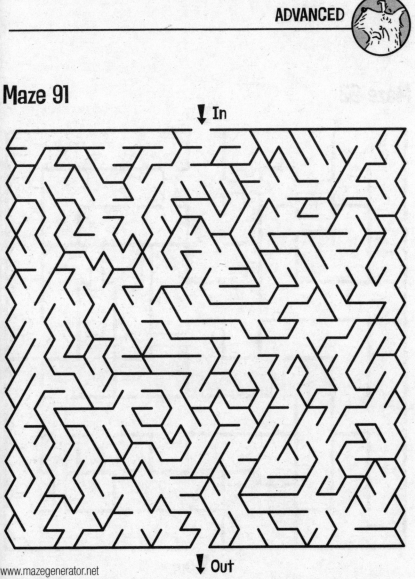

↓ In

↓ Out

Time ....

ADVANCED

Maze 92

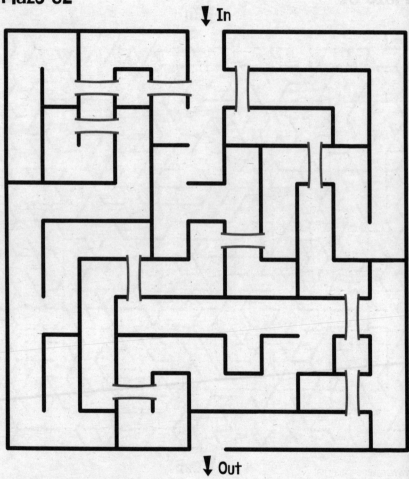

▼ In

▼ Out

Maze 93

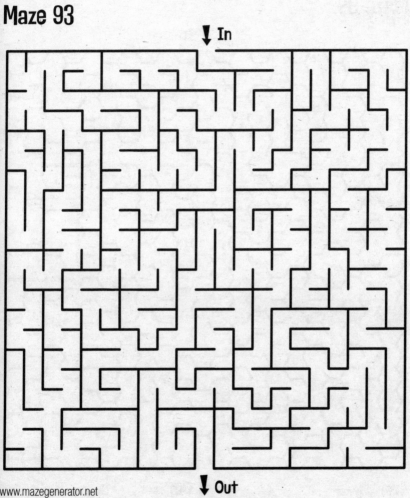

Time

ADVANCED

Maze 94

↓ **In**

↓ **Out**

 Time ....

ADVANCED

Maze 95

In

Out

Time

Maze 96

In

Out

🕐 Time ....

Maze 97

In

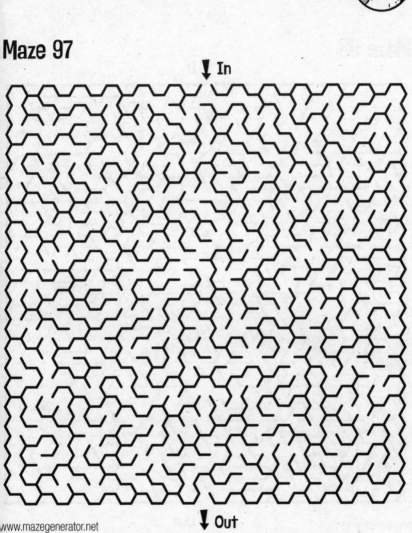

Out

Time

Maze 98

▼ In

▼ Out

 Time................................

Maze 99

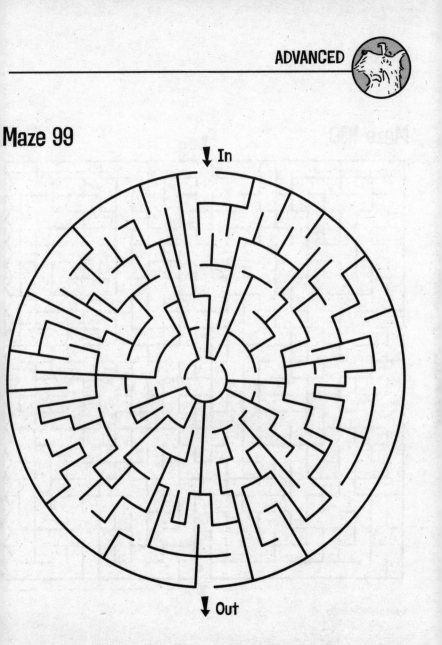

Time

Maze 100

In

Out

 Time...

Maze 101

↓ In

↓ Out

Time ....

 ADVANCED

Maze 102

↓ In

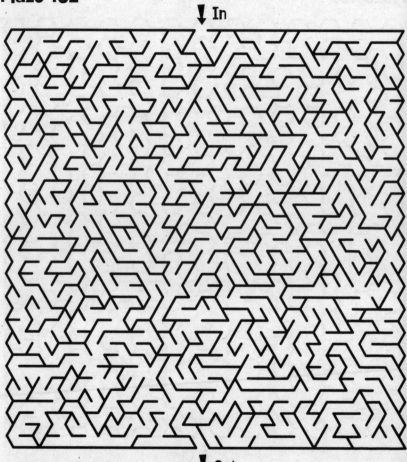

↓ Out

 Time ....

Maze 103

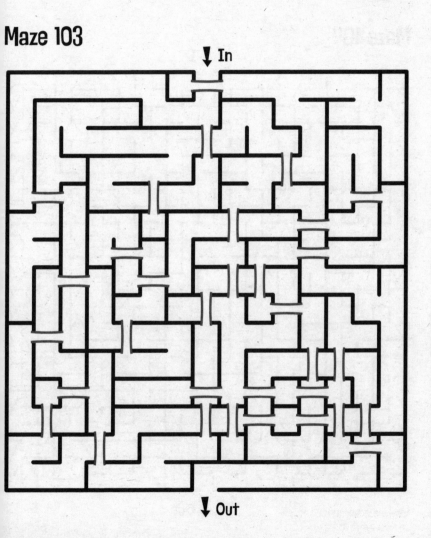

Time ....

ADVANCED

Maze 104

↓ In

↓ Out

🕐 **Time** _____

Maze 105

▼ In

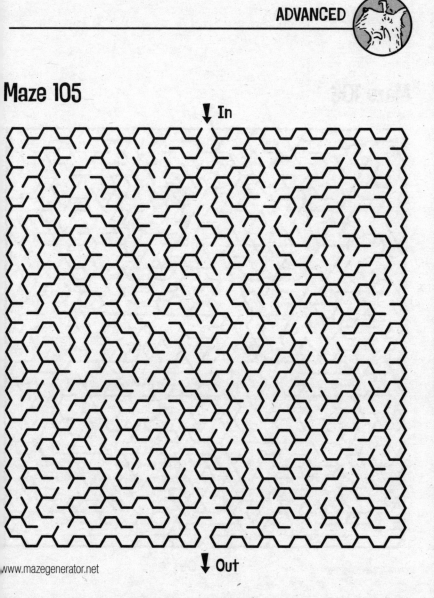

▼ Out

Time ....

 ADVANCED

Maze 106

↓ In

↓ Out

 Time ....

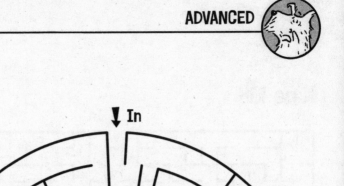

Maze 107

Time ....

Maze 108

In

Out

Time ....

Maze 109

↓ In

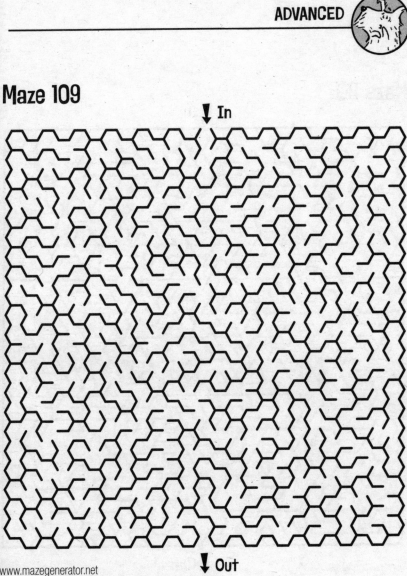

↓ Out

Time ....

Maze 110

↓ In

↓ Out

🕐 **Time** ....

Maze 111

↓ In

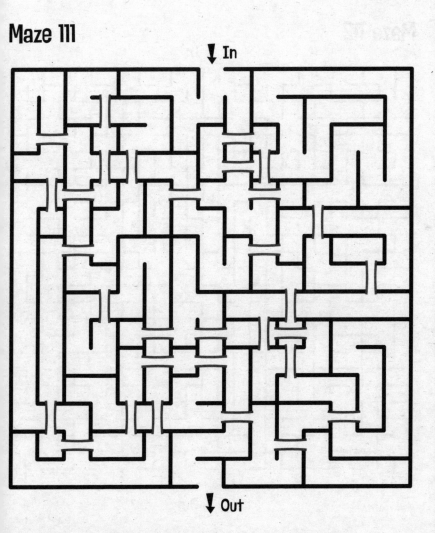

↓ Out

Time..

ADVANCED

Maze 112

In

Out

 Time ....

Maze 113

▼ In

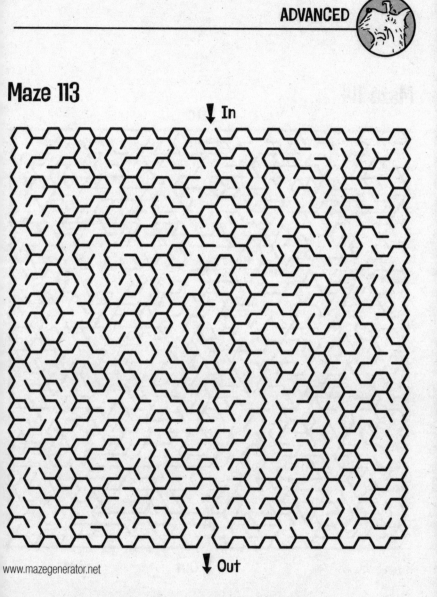

▼ Out

Time ....

Maze 114

↓ In

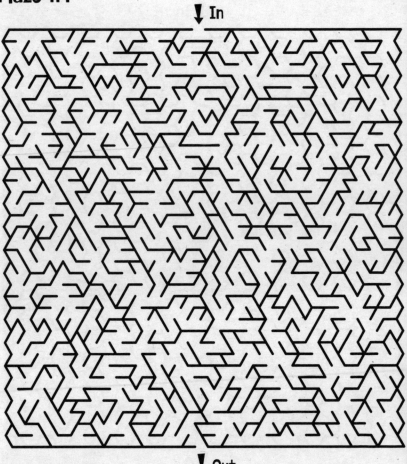

↓ Out

Time ....

Maze 115

↓ In

↓ Out

Time _____

Maze 116

In

Out

Time ....

Maze 117

↓ In

↓ Out

Time

 **ADVANCED**

Maze 118

↓ In

↓ Out

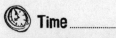 **Time** ....

Maze 119

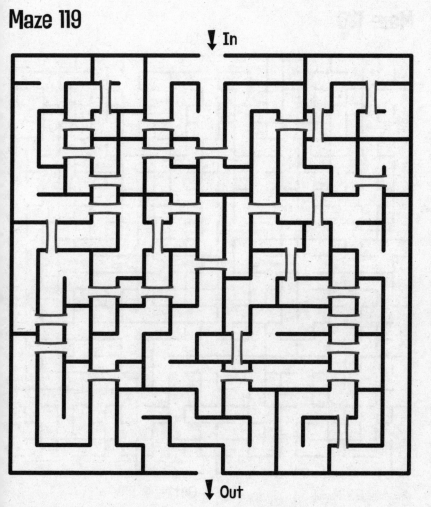

↓ In

↓ Out

Time ....

ADVANCED

Maze 120

↓ In

↓ Out

www.mazegenerator.net

🕐 **Time** ....

Maze 121

↓ In

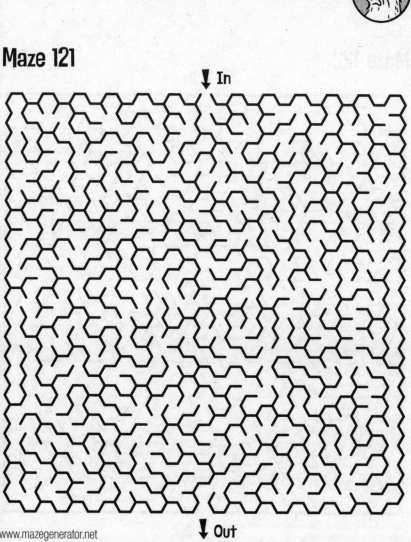

↓ Out

Time ....

Maze 122

In

Out

 Time ....

Maze 123

Time ....

Maze 124

↓ **In**

↓ **Out**

 Time ....

Maze 125

↓ In

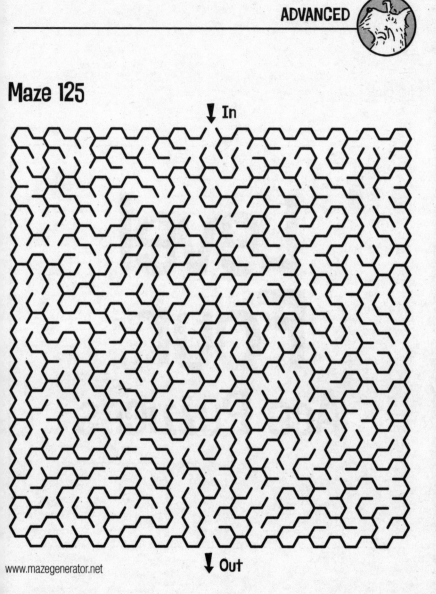

↓ Out

Time ....

Level Four:
Ace Puzzlers

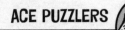

Maze 126

Time ....

Maze 127

↓ In

↓ **Out**

 Time ....

Maze 128

Time ....

ACE PUZZLERS

Maze 129

↓ In

↓ Out

 Time ....

Maze 130

In

Out

Time ....

Maze 131

↓ In

↓ Out

 Time ....

Maze 132

In

Out

Time ....

Maze 133

↓ **In**

↓ **Out**

🕐 **Time** ....

Maze 134

↓ In

↓ Out

Time

Maze 135

In

Out

 Time ....

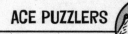

Maze 136

↓ In

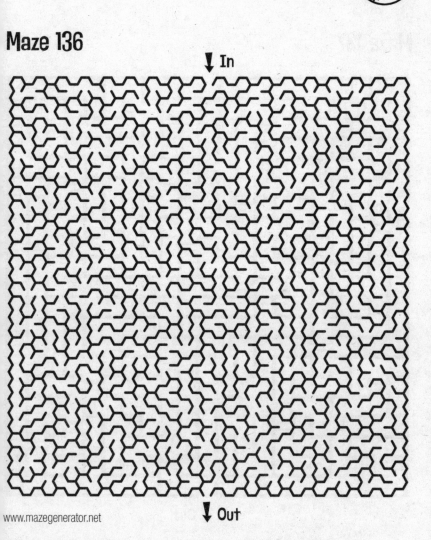

↓ Out

Time ....

ACE PUZZLERS

Maze 137

↓ In

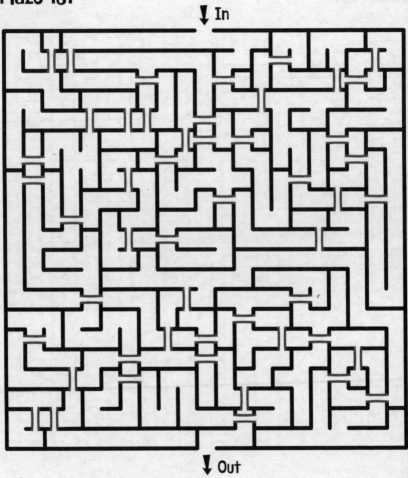

↓ Out

Time ....

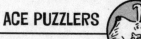

Maze 138

↓ In

↓ Out

Time

ACE PUZZLERS

Maze 139

▼ In

www.mazegenerator.net

▼ Out

🕐 Time ....

Maze 140

▼ In

▼ Out

Time ....

ACE PUZZLERS

Maze 141

In

Out

Time ....

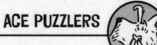

Maze 142

↓ **In**

↓ **Out**

Time ....

ACE PUZZLERS

Maze 143

↓ In

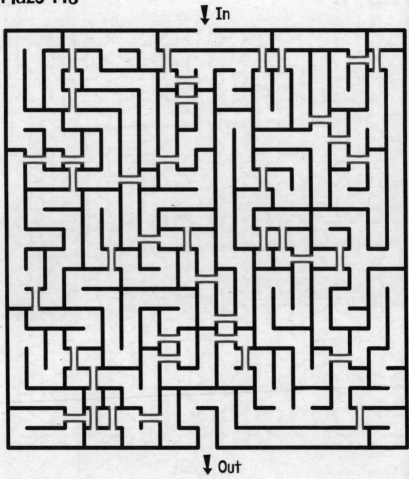

↓ Out

 Time ....

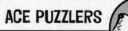

Maze 144

↓ In

↓ Out

Time ....

ACE PUZZLERS

Maze 145

↓ In

↓ Out

Time ....

Maze 146

↓ In

↓ Out

Time

Maze 147

↓ In

↓ Out

🕐 Time ....

Maze 148

In

Out

Time ....

ACE PUZZLERS

Maze 149

▼ In

▼ Out

 Time ....

Maze 150

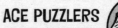 **In**

Out

Time ....

 **ACE PUZZLERS**

Maze 151

In

Out

🕐 **Time**

Maze 152

In

Out

Time.....................................

Maze 153

▼ In

▼ Out

 Time ....

Answers

Beginners

Maze 1

Maze 2

Maze 3

Maze 4

Maze 5

Maze 6

Maze 7

Maze 8

Maze 9

Maze 10

Maze 11

Maze 12

Maze 13

Maze 14

Maze 15

Maze 16

Maze 17

Maze 18

Maze 19

Maze 20

Maze 21

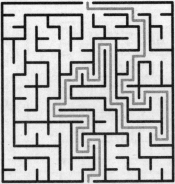

Intermediates

Maze 27

Maze 28

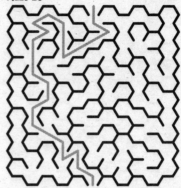

Maze 29

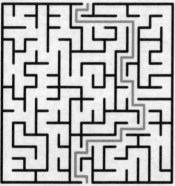

Maze 30

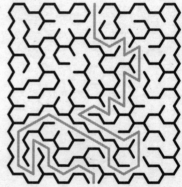

Maze 31

Maze 32

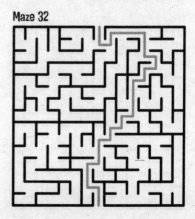

Maze 33

Maze 34

Maze 35

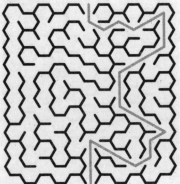

Maze 36

Maze 37

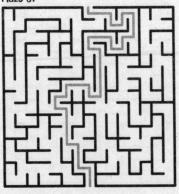

Maze 38

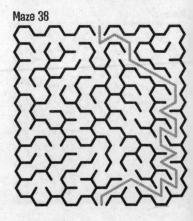

Maze 39

Maze 40

Maze 41

Maze 42

Maze 43

Maze 44

Maze 45

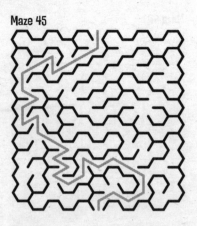

Maze 46

Maze 47

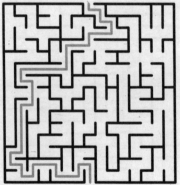

Maze 48

Maze 49

Maze 50

Maze 51

Maze 52

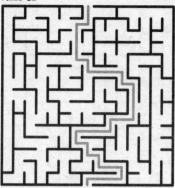

Maze 53

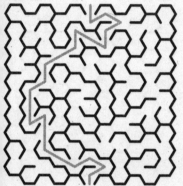

Maze 54

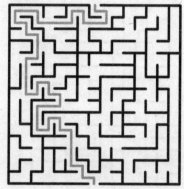

Maze 55

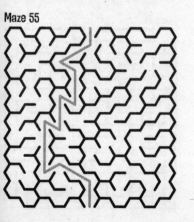

Maze 56

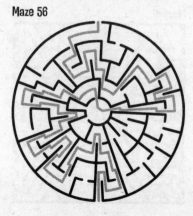

Maze 57

Maze 58

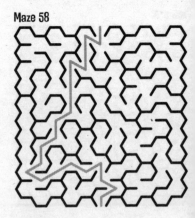

Maze 59

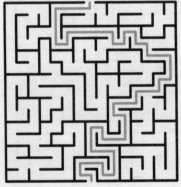

Maze 60

Maze 61

Maze 62

Maze 63

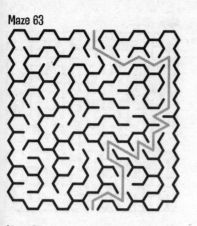

Maze 64

Maze 65

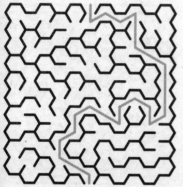

Maze 66

Maze 67

Maze 68

Advanced

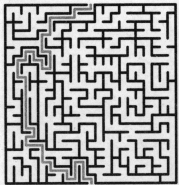

Maze 69

Maze 70

Maze 71

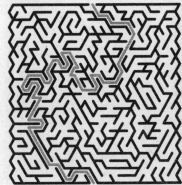

Maze 72

Maze 73

Maze 74

Maze 75

Maze 76

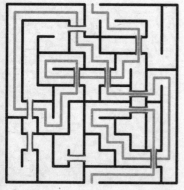

Maze 77

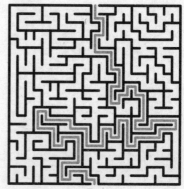

Maze 78

Maze 79

Maze 80

Maze 81

Maze 82

Maze 83

Maze 84

Maze 85

Maze 86

Maze 87

Maze 88

Maze 89

Maze 90

Maze 91

Maze 92

Maze 93

Maze 94

Maze 95

Maze 96

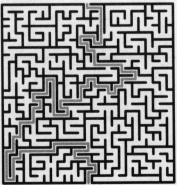

Maze 97

Maze 99

Maze 101

Maze 102

Maze 103
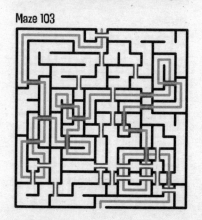

Maze 104

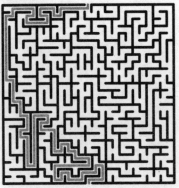

Maze 105

Maze 106

Maze 107

Maze 108

Maze 109

Maze 110

Maze 111

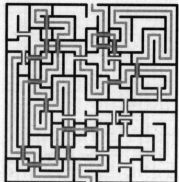

Maze 112

Maze 113

Maze 114

Maze 115

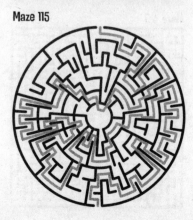

Maze 116

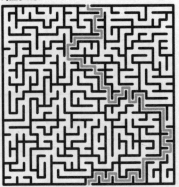

Maze 117

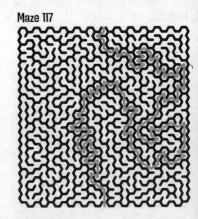

Maze 118

Maze 119

Maze 120

Maze 121

Maze 122

Maze 123

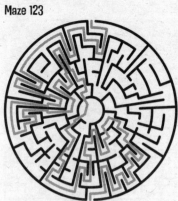

Maze 124

Maze 125

Ace
Puzzlers

Maze 126

Maze 127

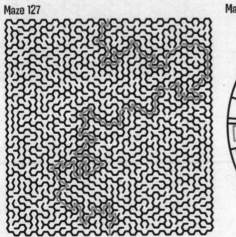

Maze 128

Maze 129

Maze 130

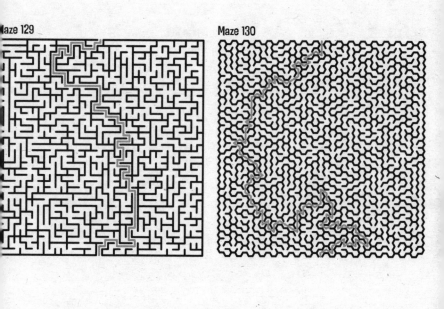

Maze 131

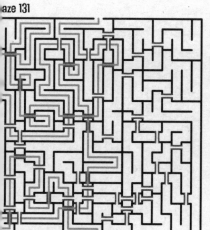

Maze 132

Maze 133

Maze 134

Maze 135

Maze 136

Maze 137

Maze 138

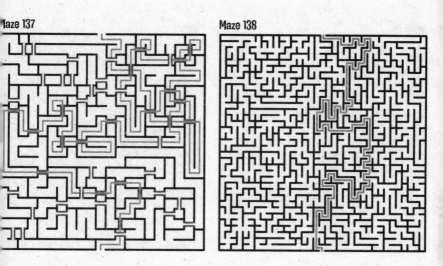

Maze 139

Maze 140

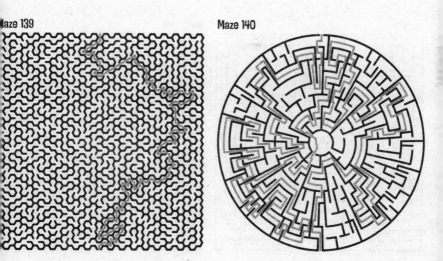

Maze 141

Maze 142

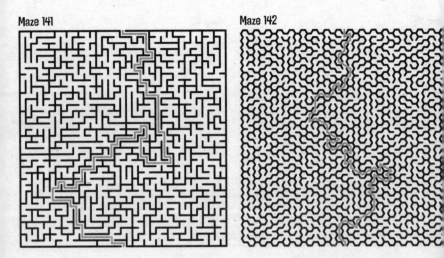

Maze 143

Maze 144

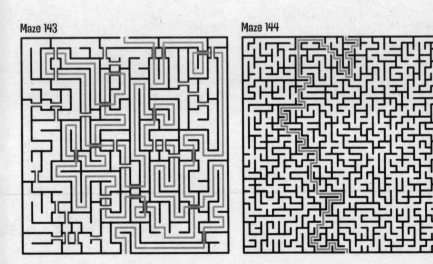

Maze 145

Maze 146

Maze 147

Maze 148

Maze 149

Maze 150

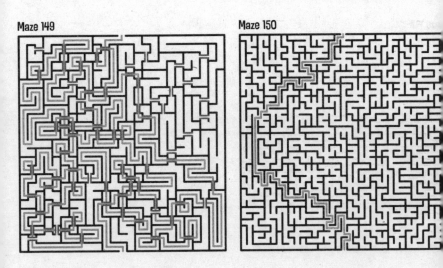

Maze 151

Maze 152

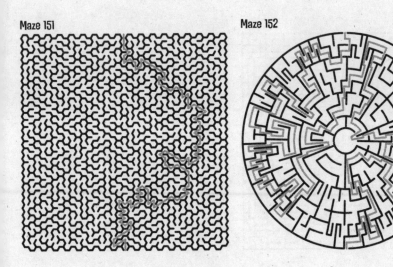